KT-442-942

THE PRINCIPLE OF WATER

Also by Jon Silkin

POETRY

The Peaceable Kingdom
The Two Freedoms
The Re-ordering of the Stones
Nature with Man
Penguin Modern Poets 7
    (with Richard Murphy and Nathaniel Tarn)
Poems New and Selected
Killhope Wheel
Amana Grass

CRITICISM AND ANTHOLOGY

Out of Battle
    (Poets of the First World War)
Poetry of the Committed Individual
    (a *Stand* anthology)

THE PRINCIPLE
OF WATER

Jon Silkin

A Carcanet Press Publication

Acknowledgements are due to the following periodicals:
Antaeus, British Poetry 1972 (The Baleen Press, Arizona), *European
Judaism, Fuse, Here Now, Iowa Review, Jewish Quarterly, New
Poetry* (Australia), *New Statesman, Orbis, Outposts, PEN 1973,
Poetry* (USA), *Poetry Book Society Supplement* (1971), *Responses*
(National Book League), *Stand, The Poet, the Review, The
Scotsman, The Valley Press* (USA), *Times Literary Supplement,
Tribune, Vanderbilt Poetry Review*.
Acknowledgements are also due to the Sceptre Press, the Scolar
Press, and to George Stephenson and the Mid-Northumberland
Arts Group for the entire *Killhope Wheel* sequence. 'The People'
produced by John Scotney was broadcast on the BBC Third
Programme, as were other poems in this collection.

I would like to acknowledge the help and encouragement of
Lorna Tracy, Rodney Pybus, Michael Schmidt, Emanuel
Litvinoff, Eric Northey and Merle Brown – though this need not
be taken to imply an unguarded liking for the poems on their part.

First published 1974
by Carcanet Press Limited
266 Councillor Lane
Cheadle Hulme, Cheadle
Cheshire SK8 5PN

Printed by W & J Mackay Limited, Chatham

4

CONTENTS

A STRAND FROM CAEDMON

Now must we praise heaven's possessor;

I cannot sing. And silent, as at first,
left the feasting.

The holy Shaper, first he fashioned

as a roof the heavens, and the middle earth
this eternal Lord, he after adorned.

I cannot sing. Silence magnifies
the creaturely, livid dross of flies
pricking faeces.
               Our almighty King,
this glorious Father, the everlasting Lord,
wrought the beginning of wonders each one.

Near the farm, voices encrusting
tree-forms of grass bitten by deer.

The air opens, the cuneiform voices
wedging praise. Also to be seen

the harrowing angel, his still wings'
extended denunciation

Killhope
Wheel

TREE

Under the yard, earth could enable nothing, nothing
opened in it. I smelt it once, when the floor
was up, disabled, rank. I made boxes
and grow mint, rhubarb, parsley
and seedlings that lift a furl of leaves, slightly
aside an unwavering stem.
A friend dragged a barrel off rocks, we took it home;
I chose a tree for it. It is five foot
with branches that may stretch across
the wall, with minute fruits, of hardly any colour.
Its leaves point open, and down. The whole tree
can glisten, or die. It is dark green
in earth mixed with peat dug by a lake
and dung I crumbled in.
I can't fudge up a relationship, but it gladdens
you, as the sun concentrates it, and I
want the creature for what it is
to live beyond me.

(UNTITLED)

Small hills, among the fells, come apart from the large
where streams drop; the water-flowers
bloom at the edges, or in the shallows, together,
and are white. Whoever comes here, comes, glad, at least
and as they look, it is with some care, you can feel
that on flower, may tree, or dry-stone wall
their gaze collects in a moist, comely pressure.
I feel this, but slog elsewhere.
Swan Hunter's is where we build naval craft;
they emerge: destroyer, the submarine
fitted, at length, by electricians. Their work
is inspected; it is again re-wired. In the heat
men walk high in the hulk on planks, one
of them tips, and he falls the depth of the hold.
It is hot. The shithouses are clagged, the yard's
gates closed for security. The food is not good.
Some people in here are maimed.
I am trying to make again the feeling
plants have, and each creature has, looked at,
demure, exultant. The man who has fallen
looks at me, and looks away.

CENTERING

At the West End, a bridge.
Coaling houses, shutes, and among such power,
contrived, at the top, a little lever
which would unclasp the heavy trap.
All the ships come for here is fuel. Few come.
And none, further.
Near the bridge, each side, houses
struggling to cross over.

More east, seawards, a further bridge.
The trains bend that way, then, turning square,
cross the whole river.
Below, the quay, meant to focus
activity to it.

The maritime offices, craft
moored from Denmark.
The masts' shadows stable on the customs sheds.

No centre can be formed
here or by the next bridge. The trains
pass on a tier above the road.

Nor here; the road belts between
the strength of the region fused into two spans,
gone.

Two precipitate banks, where water pushes
within a moment of the quick of you, bituminous
and rank.
If you were made
at the river-side
you have to be a spanning, at least.

KILLHOPE WHEEL, 1860, COUNTY DURHAM

1860. Killhope Wheel, cast
forty feet in iron across, is swung
by water off the North Pennines
washing lead ore crushed here.

And mined, here. Also fluor-spar.
In 1860 soldiers might kill
miners if they struck.

A board says that we're free to come in.
Why should it seem absurd to get
pain from such permission? Why have

I to see red-coat soldiers prick
between washed stones, and bayonets
tugged from the flesh?

Among the North Pennines what might
have seeped the flesh of miners, who chucked
their tools aside?

I can't work out what I have
come here for; there's no mineable lead
or work of that kind here now.

Why does a board, tacked to wood,
concerning my being free to visit
nourish my useless pain?

Like water. I am its water, dispersed
in the ground I came from; and have footage
on these hills, stripped of lead,

which the sheep crop, insensibly white.
The mist soaks their cries into them.

STRIKE

The earth comes moist-looking, and blackens;
a trickle of earth where the feet pressed,
twice a day, wearing off the grass.
Where the miners
were seen: a letter blown damply
into the corner of a hut: 'Oh dear love, come to me'
and nothing else.

Where are they?
The sheep bleat back to the mist balding
with terror; where
are they? The miners
are under the ground.

A pale blue patch of thick worsted
a scrag of cotton;
the wheel is still that washed the pounded ore.
They were cut down.

Almost turned by water, a stammer of the huge wheel
groping at the bearings.
Their bayonets; the red coat
gluey with red.

The water shrinks
to its source. The wheel,
in balance.

SPADE

George Culley, Isaac Greener?

A want of sound hangs
in a drop of moisture from the wheel that
turned and washed the ore.

A rustling of clothes on the wind. The water does not move.

I have come here to be afraid.
I came for love to bundle
what was mine. I am scared
to sneak into the hut to find your coat.

When you put down your pick,
when others wouldn't sprag
the mine's passages; when you said no:

soldiers, who do not strike,
thrust
their bayonets into you.

They were told to.

The young mayor, shitting, closeted
with chain on his neck. I want to

push my hands into your blood
because I caused you to use yours.

I did not die; love, I did not. All the parts
of England fell melting like lead away,
as you showed me the melting once, when you and the men
with you were jabbed,

and without tenderness, were filled over;
no psalm, leaf-like, shading the eyelid
as the eye beneath is dazed abruptly
in the earth's flare of black light
burning after death.

The spade digging in the sunlight illuminates the face of my
                    God.
Blind him.

(UNTITLED)

Concerning strength,
it is unequal. In a paddock
by Stakeford, slag, with bushes dripping
over stone, a horse crops, slowly, his strength
tethered into the ground. The Wansbeck
shivers over the stone, bits of coal, and where
it halts a pool fills, oily
and twitching. Closer to the sea, it drops
under a bridge, coming to ground
where the mind opens, and gives uselessly to
the sun such created heat, the air
cleaves to the flesh,
the bench facing the water, sat on by old men.
If this goes, nothing; this clearness
which draws a supple smell through old skin
making a pause for it. Houses and scrap will heap,
and flake, as
if organs of the soil clagged
with shreddings of rust.

PLATELAYER
(for J. M.)

'I did not serve, but was skilled
for fifty years, laying plates
measured as carefully apart
as seedlings.' The line came
west from Morpeth, crossing
the third road for Scotland.
At Knowesgate, four houses
group on a bank, set away.
A station was built there.
'I laid plates for eight miles,
but short of Morpeth, sledging chucks
that held the rails; kept them so,
although this has gone now.
Yet here are four pines of
the five I put in. And here
I helped to concrete that
that was the goods bay.
My dog has sixteen years.
We both suffer the heat.
And yet her owners had said
that she must be put down.
I did not say that. And the lupins
strike through the platform;
with a better chance I think
they'd have not done well.
But what I think is that
my work was finished up: five years
past the track taken apart.
No, not so; now we've cranes
to hoist the lengths that we
laid down, form on form. Also gone
a certain friend, who finished
when I was made free.
I shan't work any job
twice. And this is strange,
having the letter from the man,
although it was not him.

17

Yet surely as like him
as the bolts drove in.
"I can't think of your name
or what you are. You must
excuse me and I have
nothing to tell you and
why I am shut up here
I can't speak of with nothing
to speak about."
But still I am certain
the track we built was skilled,
although you can't tell that.'

'THE BIRD IS LIGAMENTED. . .'

The bird is ligamented without a soul; it is lifted
in a wind, blasted from the silica furnace.

The
People

A Pennsylvania German Pie Plate

Hand-wrought-and-decorated in 1786 it is inscribed, 'The plate is made of clay; when it breaks, the potter laughs.' When he's dead even. He turns over as it breaks, and laughs; unless he, like the plate, has baked in the oven.

Pray thee, take care, that tak'st my book in hand,
To reade it well: that is, to understand.
                                        – Jonson

ONIRIQUE

FINN

I melt to sleep on my left side
and dream
of archaic beasts, baring a white honed smile;
unpunishable, alert, and pacified
in mutual consent, their quirked grins knit
a peaceable, brilliant continuum.
Which goes.

Branches are cut, and cross-piled in a square
to eat the flesh up of a heretic.
Each has a defined
nick in it; but why
I ask.

On my right side I dream how
by an inn, God molests
a tired man, austerely erect.
And cleaves the flesh, but that those halves each time
melt whole again.

Once you've the knack, I shout, the fun in it will come.

A dry voice answers that what I say is
more in its line. Like death, I say. And it:
you're not about to die yet, nor is he.

My God, I thought, that is as well. I am not
about to find
any screwball
sticking by me.

'You're premature' the voice said. I got dandled
onto a cleft in rock. The voice disposed
no face, no comfort I might draw from it.

But as in a dream felt
the hand, fitting
that one likewise upon a shelf, as if

but bored, too
much with it

moved off.

Brief dream. But under the cut pile
of branches, an odour
of soiled, fouling life

more murderous than this God

gorgeous with light

that light incised by smiles
at the teeth's edge, by men
turning to stare at it.

I turn, waking, and reach for Kye who sleeps
in first pregnancy. I catch
up my breath and kiss her.

I GROWING

FINN

A dog howls over stubble fields, where smoke
wavers between two straight trees;
no sounds billow frost-marked hedgerows.
Yet he uses distance, his bark dispersing
as smoke in the lull after harvest before spring,
that taints, by London, the country air.
I turn off to where my wife will labour soon,
gravid in blood, spinal nerve. And quit
heavy winter sharpness, with sullen empty light
reddening grass-tips, hair on fruits' skins.
What is at home? No sound mixes the door's
jarring its hinge. A voice. Yes, I answer.
Each thing here is childbirth. Metal bowls
cambered like shallowed buttocks, the heavy slope
of another is her stretched belly in the weighed
drop to her cunt, that opens. She calls.
The pouting track's soft firmness dilates;
jugs gleam, wide-lipped, prepared for dropping
water to grin in lolloping mirth; the stable, working pan
will get the flow bent onto the wheel turning
to wash the pounded ore.
Come up love, Kye asks. The stone and wood room
having winter flowers, a fire banters
its tongues onto their erect blue flare.
One other is here, her friend, large-boned: sit, she says,
in your own house. Laughs. He'll not be long.
How do you know 'he'? we each ask her.
By his size, by that, with his slow turning
about. But there's the kettle, and ring the nurse.
Kiss me, Kye asks. Her brow gathers
moisture in the furrows, ploughman's sweat.
I wipe her and kiss her.
                         Below, fire heaves
behind iron, intently heating a pot
and sinks into itself, moulting ash.

Its vitality itches terror into the wood it eats;
flesh deciduates in passion. I love this girl,
who is making our child. The nurse comes;
her stiff apron is white and terrorful.
I am upstairs, Kye asking to hold to me. Warmth
beats across her fear and mine. Her fear
is of what makes in her, mine's a white subtraction.
Yet she holds to me, as I touch that swollenness.
'Now' she quivers 'he stretches me, love.'
'Now hangs back in me.' Yes, a hump,
and sullen, feeling no joy rooted here. But we
wait for its first shove, as it is
to issue rushing, cord knotted, cut,
and reversed into the navel. 'Now' she breathes. If she
pushes, I can't tell if he does, or it's she.
'Hold me,' she insists, 'no, don't.' Fastens to my wrist. I suffer
no hand, but its grip. Sweat shakes off again.
Her bowels move, and open. Then at the parting
of strange lips,
her child, clustering, heaves a gulf open. She pushes,
now contracts, heaves wider, and it is going to come.
It is. 'No.' A pause, renewed, for its coming,
rushing out. Has it? It does, and the spiral wreck
of abdominal life terminates, the creature stirring it.
Even as he's lifted, lightly slapped
for his first cry, I know I shall not
see him unnamed again.

Kye, for his necessity, from hair to feet
is specked and salt, its glistening
moist as placental amnion.
Now it is, for cleansing, the water's turn. Poured,
capable and clear, into the cool, a milky
fluid dripped precisely, and her body washed; never
as helplessly lying, cleaned of excreta and blood.
Sponged gently. As grass is plaited in a crown
for the May's queen, queen not of herself
but of each one's May; as, blithely, in equal parts
each of us is the May, so she is washed.

He howls. 'That's hunger. Pick him up, here,
he is yours.' The nurse smiles. Lines in her small face
crease her labour, with others', on her;
midwife to each child she lifts him to Kye's breast.

First food passes his mouth;
then he lies quiet, and is knit to her
in such sticky entangling he will unpick.
                                      For now, the arm
grows large she holds him in. Cinders stir.
A dog barks, splintering light.
The pans are hard at rest, we would be glad for as much.
                                      Coldness stands up
and, full of care, puts both arms
about the solid house.

                              At eighteen,
my first journey, at length, though not specially,
with one pain. Opening gates,
the signal, its painted alpine station, with beyond
numberless circumscription.

I've my circumcision,
with, in Riga,
the same shit:
loathing, the gentile's
stare backward.

It comes, love, again;
we are to be plucked, much
as the mouth, fastened on pain
rejects its tooth.

England, a stable calm,
crosses the road. I am
a step from me to those
two whom I love. But then?

I am a great way off from anything.

A wind reverses each cloud through the boughs,
notching the tips of this adjacent moon.
A nimbus incompletely haloing.
                              Past this
third house, I see a neighbour. A light wind
tightens her skirt above her knees, tanned lightly,
and creased. She is political, she says,
and, formed inside the party, used, who would
be used, taking from her her youth, as if
a ghost despondent of its flesh. It is
the cause. Is it? For now, perplexities
in certainty creep onto the small mouth,
tampering the vigour prompting its bare skin,
that wears as anxious to prove serviceable.
Ruthlessness pauses lightly, knowing to get

and score her generosity away
it seems, until the bone is at its skin.

Stares at a number sweated
into my shirt;
naked, I'd swathe my wrists.

She has no child, and I,
in me, spores of grief
shield their eyes.

More flesh: the furnace eats,
and sweats dust.

Columnal fierceness of some brilliant march
from Egypt's swamp or grit. We undo the bland
obedient waters of the flat red sea,
the hovering walls, balancing God's natureless signs.
Bad nerves thread distant, but avenging, forms
displaced, a time, by God's mild crucial hands.
Burnished armour, and strength stepping in it,
this crosses to some locus where its face
is crossed upon another, glimmering
in iron. Each pays.
In Europe, the Jews
pay definitively.

Lying in Buchenwald, as the British moved
up to us
in slinging densities of ash, one man
walked, dressed in brown, through it, and lifted me
up in his arms. I felt like a mild plant,
shame cringing me. But he was crying. That one
should be cried for, as if a plant had worth
beyond its fruit and serviceableness;
outside the staked wire, heaps a pit, and spaced
an equal area from two further ones;
a mass grave, and the indifferent botany
of herbs branching a pungent sullenness.

Those whom I touched, I left. No weeping,
that salt drawn as in work, sweat fiery
through labour, frozen
bolting fuselages

with her who ceased.

Why should I not have been born as a word
sprawling inside a Yiddish lexicon.

I cried 'love' once; no person answered it.

I visit my friends now,
their house, rooted
under a hill of cropped grass, and by
a farm: Adam
and who made him.

Finn and Kye

What is it that will not eat mash from a bowl?
that lets the spoon come to its lips, then ails
and weeps, or, if the spoon pries past them,
weeps and chokes? Or being fed
vomits his mash entire.
Earlier, as if that mesh of him were
my making only, and that he won't eat
my care alone, and I could, alone, unpick
his belly's tightening
she flung him on his back, hard, over the bed.
He lay astonished. Then huge tears swelling with
the eyelids, came away from him. Silence
breaking with moisture on his cheeks.
I felt what he might learn. Much anger, bruised
in hatred, he got thrust down with. From me,
his wetness on my stubble, cowed by her
that he could see. Deliberately, she asks,
why is he silent, and, why does his food
not stay with him; what is his quietness?
I can't reply. She smiles: it is as if,
she answers, he's made perfectly. As if.
As though perfectly made, but in him, life
moves very little – love, it is not there.
Then hesitantly, but then, instantly sure
she lifts him,
holding him to her with such tenderness the slight
widths of air between them, as she slowly brings
him to her, yield and tense in supple
passion endured by both. Instantly
he cries to her, long, slow, insistent, rising
to screams, as he tenses his head from her.
She lulls him, his pained flesh swaying her with him.
It is as if, she says, pausing, in him
nothing joins. As if that tissue in us
that forms an Adam, or a Finn, has not
met in him.

I might tell him; but how might I, blithely
as my lips on his penis, or as
with brimmed a softness on his quick as it
is tight in him? Why won't my sweet intent
not pass from me to him, as I took in
his well-planted, minute, sturdy seed?
I want the child to take breath into him.
Yet how, love, – where, I'm asking, in him is
the tangled sense laid
as nerve-web in the well-held inner bowl,
a bowl supping the discontinuous
splashes of shape and feeling on him, that form
the memory that is him.

She tilts her head; a grin, being obdurate,
edges the eye and mouth sharply. Some mirth.

I am, yet what I am no man has touched.
I was made slenderly, you know; and fleshed
over the buttocks.
My hair is long, and light, and hangs.
My head draws at the back into a curve
that implicates a mind webbed in a brain.
My fingers are long, and small, and my waist
tucks in over my hips. Two men
were there before you, and no other one.
Yes, but this should not flatter you, for here
I exercise my choice. Love, oh my love,
you touch my breasts and they excite. You kiss
my flesh as if you loved me. But my lips
force a smile sometimes I do not half-mean.
I loathe this. My mind is not dainty; tough,
perhaps, and pert pert as a bean, yet, so,
irregular. Love, if we do connect,
we have a child fresh as a white berry –
I speak no more of it; what we have made
is beautiful, I know; and tenderness
will sour in me if your neat courage deserts.
Whatever he will make, he should grow soon
my literate intelligence, with it

your shrewd imagination, sharp as sand
and newly cut, edging the mind's thin blades.
He should have – love, lift him, and see if you
find in him our minds, joined up in that new,
that lithe, unbaulked, hurtling intelligence
so beautiful to see; see, there, I think I felt it.

II HISTORY

1. STEIN

I tailored three suits, which hang
empty of me.

Come kitty come on kitty
                              my three
cats
wail in a curve formed
on each other. And leap on.

A string vibrating three
versions of one plucked self

    Some life goes on
    no one said it would not.

2. STEIN

A tale-bearer
                    treads the horizon
and we converge.
Asking: which emperor
                              did Tacitus loathe?
History has limits.

I write down nothing of experience
I was combed through, like the head-louse.

I made up nothing
                        from others' print
nor satisfied
                  the need for some key-figure

but in extremity budded
                              and was pressed
between leaves. I made up
history in the lump

holding it in me.
And what of that I was I can bring
upwards constantly. No wreath of judgments
pricking my forehead.
                    Uncertainly I'll promise
to bring an opinion, after I am dead,
as a mild ghost stirs benevolent for talk
on earth, beside a steaming hearth-fire.

The numbers stamping
                    my wrists
derive no mystical insight
                    and, if seen
will not touch a soul.

I wear what is marked on me. Suffering is not strength
wanting,
        or down-payment
                    on survival;
if it implicates
            spiritual qualities,
that's accident. In the pitiers, even so
pity in action is dead.
                    I survived
drinking my wife's urine.
                    And again,
the rifle's thud.
            Additionally
a foot burned, the death of every beloved:
many in there were beloved.

Oh my love, virtue was not dropped
from between God's thumb and finger.
As we went for it, the shell husked
small droppings from the worm, as if
who should be virtuous.

Problems heap in amongst the remnant.
In each case men say 'He is a Jew'.
                    One says

'Jew' in Israel, implanting their difference.
For whose sake, 'Their deaths must not
diffuse through mud.' Who is mud, I ask.
Our monument's barb
                    steadies in rock
Jerusalem is
              a stone over.
I'm not yet dead;
                  others may have wished
intimate remembering.

How how? Monuments
                    absent the mind
excuse it, are not
ruth, not pity, nor sinewy discourse
in the here or to-come of us.

Again my life
              fines to a point
pressing here

on four of us. Kye breathes
in this place edged by fields.
A tree that sides their house
taps at the glass and scrapes
thick spicy leaves onto
transparent barriers,
chill and brittle. She is
as if my daughter once
removed in blood; she smiles
and nods, but fitfully,
on my words. Adam, not
not my child but take in
a deeper breath, love, than
you have done yet, and touch
my mind, as Finn touches
the child in me.
What is to come, I want
to know, of me and them?

3. STEIN

If my people were to forgive the enemies of my people there would be no forgiveness for my people. Mother, Mother!

III TESTING

FINN

These are London's consiliary
offices of stone, edging
the river with a prospect of
not flowers, pilasters of hope

in bloom. Each stone face is firm
with rhyme, and echoing a confidence
borrowed. Rectangular stone widths
group upon the forecourt

disdaining the river. A lower wall
silvers tidally, with, in traces
the sediments of us, dirt
the dried skin of London, forced
off into the stream.

The way to enter is
through front doors; we are
going to, with Adam, for
doctors, whose tests

relieve ourselves each
of hope and, with it,
unhoping care.

No trees; water that
is to the building
what the building is.

And we who caused it, in
whose service it is –
and those who work in it
stained with tea, compose

a fleshless soul, the extremity
of service,
of utter purity, slightly
gone off.

Mother, Mother! these buildings
with us in them, integers
zealously conflated in the common good.

The common-wealth magnified
by each of its hand-servants
to the power of one.

KYE

We have sat four hours, with Adam,
that tests may be made
added into such choice
he can't know we make.

The trailing corridors, lights regularly
spaced between mahogany doors. One is
opening for us.
Adam feels cold, sweating lightly.
The temperature is lowering; the anxious
chronometrication of London's business
in this slight chill, where we live
netted in its jurisdiction.
Adam is sweating, coldly. Almost a year.
In the marble jamb a fossil
unfolds a shape we enter.

KYE

Up on his toes, it is amazing how,
the man creeps from behind our son, and brings
before him a huge bell, clanging it hard.
Adam continues smiling. On the couch,
naked and tranquil, no jolt of his breath
until, a minute after, a thick sigh
dismaying the held silence, shakes out.
Startles us. But not him, nor him. A bell
with no responsiveness to it. A sigh
shaken out from the child's watched silences
elapsing then, definitively shuts
this winter's interview.

What silence, with what effort. The ringed finger
barring the lips, his voice quavers through phlegm
blown off the lungs, the ejaculatory
opinion, fined by logic down – the forms
imaging science, and colourless as dew.
The earth breathes out. The business, as is normal,
shut into words that close the test. The tone
is natural, and sparkles decently
with worth; the nifty instruments replaced
unneeded as unused; writing is done
niched in behind a desk, as London's madness like
the waters of the Thames through London's council drifts,
and is checked.
                    We feel,
in glances, relieved, his work certified. But Adam
is proscribed. And we
being young, with no further obligation, entered
upon the state, its ample lap, its breast
moistening him.

It is what I have done. I feel, used by
using these instruments, what this man feels.
Adam with smiles is grasping seriously
the adult finger in his palm. Is love,
using this knowledge, love? let it lie there.

This is the letter, which the hospital
will take him in with. Leave him there. And try,
with that life in you both, to grow whole with
a second child, but not identically,
I mean. He stops. Conceive another life
since that is what you must. Rises, and stares
over the oiled, and sliding wateriness
whose soiled dispersions pour onto Vauxhall.
What may I say? I do not know the words
of comfort for you. Goodbye; his outstretched hand
the nails round, their moons lightly white,
a circular cleanliness. I pick Adam up
weighing as much as I, smiling again.
Give me the letter, I say; Finn gives it.

FINN

Air that pricks earth with life, and turns as it
returns to darken, in the year's midnight,
thins in a chill distraction. Winter sun
burns a low arc through the horizon and
is absent. As we trudge the area where
our child is lying, this soil is trodden by
the mad, who, at the next spring, that is
at the next, may, with its flexible sense
elide by that stark light the vacancies
in their maimed circuits. If no world unfolds
these dead may rise to, if the flower half buds
a flesh that does not know itself, and does
not open in a separate flowering,
and touches signs which touch without a trace
of healing correspondence, in this world
will have to do. She, who drifts with her group
of friends, as if we beckoned, leaves, and is
behind us both. Her shape bends gently down.
Her large quiet hands, her breasts hardly there,
an independent mildness, at the mouth,
branched past the cheekbones, brushes to the eyes
widening in hunger.
She gazes, and lifts my hand up slowly to
her lips; then kissing it, releases me
with care, gently, and leaves. That gentleness
forming, without submission, as she kisses
my hand gravely – who shared in that kiss –
in which instant sane or defective; shame
at my dividing question. Walk a bit
on to the ward. Out of its souring brick,
bird-like, the mad alight, shake, and fold in
their movements to their bodies, gazing queerly,
or quiver in recognition, timid, but pressing
on us to touch us over our hands, or faces,
or touch us with their eyes; while everywhere
their mild untrained gaze forms the unsure part
in creaturely connection. And as I feel
her hand, earlier forms shed their flesh, leaving

this bare. Twelve almost, to test
my sanity, I squatted on the pavement
and put a marble on my tongue, closing
my mouth on it. If I could swallow this
and die, I was insane. Or if I left
it balancing on my tongue, then I was mad
to do this. Our child for them is mad.
We reach the twilit ward. Adam lies in
a bed as if an adult. Through his face
his blood, making the skin chill, dampening it,
stirs. He breathes, yielding a changed breath.
We labour it, and press it, the lungs
that can't be relieved, letting it from them.
She rises, and slowly, as she brings her mouth
to him, her lips widen. Lightly, and light,
as if she were withdrawing, as she sinks
beside his silence breathing, she lifts up
his head, and lightly kisses his eyelids,
his mouth, then, as she puts her finger to
his palm, turning his head to us. The eyes,
eyes that are firm, breath in a changing form
moves through them, with a flickering softness in
its shape. Over and not obscuring that,
the moisture of his body
swelling the eyes, and widening them, brings
the life that concentrates, searching itself,
to grow connections in him. Forming him,
formed, and held like this, it connected us
to him, holding us until
that moisture pressed with a thick
movement from him

IV THE CHAIR

Kye

                              Adam's chair is cut
in lions as arms. An amphora unfolds
a vine that flows up, straight, enticing to it
two massive birds, within whose wood beaks
a wooden leaf is shared, linking the chair's
wide back. Two griffons, standing, weight their front legs
over the higher branches. It seems dead
to me; no, it is threatening, and I must
move it.

My fingers stitch; a pink
nubile obedience silks
its floral vacancies.

A mimic pause between us, then – all this
bores me, Finn adds. He lifts a glass up
and, with a little shrug, releases it.
Crash. It does bore me.
                              Branches in bud
outside the pane, touching, with dried bloods.

Yesterday where in the war bombs split
I stooped in the mud: a can with rain in
advancing rust.

He does not now hear, causing me to wane
against his ear. I love him yet, and loathe
what in me's teased the vulnerable. But watch
the muscle tighten, with the flickering
under the eye, signing a violence.
Not that he'll see, I flinch. He waits, he pauses,
and lets me be. A precious flow of joy
through me, then shame at this. But more comes from him:

the house seems barely ours, is passage
through which our loneliness drifts; with nothing else
I would still want the chair. And I would watch
it squatting, four-legged, in a ploughed-up field.
So much, I think, for images, and am sharp
and hard inside me, listening to him
say we cannot avoid our pain
                              can't we,
I ask. We can do more.
                              Perhaps, he says
and will, I tell him. It is our pain, which
we cause each other, or, do not. I had
the labour, the stretched terminal closenesses to
our child. And that suffices; nothing in me
created it
                    we did, he says
                              then I
do not remember it
                    or anything,
he answers. And cuts off the music there.
A dried tune, in the head, is thwarting me.
All happens then. He slides the chair to me
hands clenching it, white as the face behind
the spaces in between the birds and vine
that light onto the garden he stares at
unseeing.
                    Sit there, he says. But I do not.
Sit there, he says, or is this dead too?
Is it? A pause. If it is, watch me then.

What may I answer, and must watch, to see
him raise it. As he lifts, the facial muscles
fasten a little glare, that switches through
the neck; he lifts, pauses, and swings the chair
against the wall. What then? Twice, I think, twice
and smashes it. I hear it splintering.
The flapping birds drop through the torn vine
rasping its leaves; the fruited, clustering vine
and tendrils spread upon them, each of these
winces apart, with every imaginable

46

tenderness we had our marriage-day.
And lie, flinching. I will not see. My face
weeps in my hands; salt is one white, death makes
another in us, by our child. I was born
weeping, into this.

Treading the snow, and pausing at a shape
to scrape it clear, a man is trying for
hard wood to make a chair from. The lane crunches.
Snow squeals. And images of war move in the snow
raising a commune recessed in the brain –
traces of snout, vixen's teeth, crab, us
smeared through the cells the mind remembers in.
The chair plants its four legs, and grows; it is
not shaped like men cut down, with sprinkled frost
tipping stubble, but a harmonious
and peaceable clop of feet treading work on.
Scrimmage of tensions in the mind form by
yielded accession on these images,
made solid in a mind perching a bird.
Chipped out, and in, creatures appear, and join
a pact; archaic ferocities remain.

Now's wood for winter fires. He took the chair
and broke it easily.
                    Stammering naive blood
was loosed once more, the little mounds of dead
snowed over. And no blood there. Here the flesh
delights to die, teasing the appetite
with helplessness, dropping into itself.
A synergy of claws agreed to meet
and lie in mildness. This went with the chair.
Teeth sheared the mild flank. All that again.
He saw, or did not; broke it, anyhow.
And no restraint, or compact, stayed. The chair'd
no strut, or style; austere harmoniousness,
simple to break. Reluctant of itself,
he broke it, and each creature so detained
by art, free with its all-eyed strength, sniffed, stepped
and tore, its one eye splinteringly glazed
over the panting flesh, whose piteousness
sheared in a mouth of spikes. These two unclasp.
Pink, with no use, their torn selves want their halves,

whose heap of neatly sphinctered grains of soil's
a small exuded heap for burial in.

My eyes sweat, watching. The blow thuds across
the leafed-out woods. A scream ends in screaming,
folding the violated air round it.
The scream, the testicles, are leafed out.

It is done, and they tell you it is done.
'Duty', they say, and 'fearful for us'.
A snap-shot of the scene, wafer and host,
as nourishment. The mind tenses and arches
a rancid gaze over its phantasies.

There is no language, some say, that could speak
of this. And some, no language that should speak.
Hush. Pure language, language must be clean
of blood. A fine incontinence of love
will not indulge the sufferers. Then wheesht.
Language is pure, has autonomy,
a life not to be tainted, and its sense
has pure separation from the thing
referred to. Words choose, and they do not choose
a moral valency for blood. And others
'save me, save me', they stammer, who reject
the blade they would not use. Tendernesses
runnel these folk together milkily;
the bitter herb regales a rawer flesh.
And again, language, they claim, tarnishes
lugging the obscene weight. A great steel
from its self gleaming, keeps its inner life
pure of rusts. Wipe it. Faintly I hear
more of this, but not much. A tiny cough.
The throat flicking its ease; dust from a coat,
a ledger of the saints, flick, it is gone.

See, it darts. Quick, firstlings come. Grasp them
before they vanish. Threads that gossamer
I did not spin. Take firm, gentle hold.
Use us, these forms repeat; as I am, so

shall they be. My past at the junction with
their separating lives, I must use quickly.
Guards coughing; the cold bore down their words; I lived.
I should make that mean something, if for those
whose lives despair. I will try.

FINN

In my own room, I am, in paint, anxious to prove
all feeling survives its facts

STEIN

1.
As if I were
their copula

as if

2.
if if

Nausea

nausea
of me

nausea

KYE

So that I must,
therefore, unpick
our marriage.

Death has crumpled Adam. This man does not like me.

And with that other man,
he will love me, not not
at all but if
I touch my husband.

What is this?

and

I cannot be forgiven my child's death I did not make.

Merely, that man would forgive me.

God, thou shrike, who
at me pried, pert
as a bean, I had
not even an orifice you wanted
but a slit
you probed in me.

I forgive you
not much.

A woman sweats God
out of her

and

the garment is, in halves,
laid by.

When death is a guest, those relatives sit in mourning (shiva) for seven days; candles are lit and burned through, it being sacrilege to extinguish them.

STEIN

They must, for our needs
cleave, as my words will
together
   the curved spirts,
its spray, the impulses
of the fountain
     folding
into their provident source

in this instance, pain.

A candle burns its white
deep-seated thread, the wax
of hot soft light shrinking
into itself. I have saved
a remnant, the terse stub
of this light which cut light
over the murdered through
the dark there, for myself.
I save it to deplore
what I have lost, and as
it finishes, I will be
a pool of hardened wax
wanting thread on a plate
whiter than me.

So then there is no point
in telling anything.
I need light for this and
need such, as will not last
beyond this, to outlast
itself, that I may live
from it. But then
the simple gout will flick

its spot of fat into
my sight, and drop in through
its dark.

I should do this – insert
a history of leaves, torn,
lifted, turning in air,
then softly
dropped, where
ground banked and pressed us
under its fall
          that two
unloving animals
find mercy's image: love

for my reasons also

in their house.

V CAMPS

STEIN

As each of you sits, hear me, please.

Which is, two images. A town clustering
over a stable bluff; of desultory
brown rough clay, and stone. Houses light up
above the river's tidal gleam, unslips
ocean merchantmen in on the sea.
In gear, tugged; blithely salt spirals off
the stable wave-form prow. Prepared enough.
Pointed north-east into the Barents sea.
The second is a park, bedded and clipped.
Laurels unfurl loose bloom. A bench in wood
upturned, its short iron legs uselessly stiff
and pointed upwards. Screwed into its back
'for Aryans only', on a metal strip.
Closed wagons are drawn in line through wind, and stop.
A melted cry behind a sealed door.
Some hush. More then, then, more, and more. The train
jerked on its wagons, covering them with
its steamy patch of roar, billowing the park.

It came. The Polish engine, sweating, among cold;
its steam breathed over snow. Wagon doors
pinioned back. Mostly the guards with dogs stood,
as we filed in. Patience, and our murmur, wavering.
Neither the young, nor the elderly, wept. Once, a guard
gently helping up an old man who faltered.
Some vomit, softly, in lumps, falling past the edge
of a wagon. Prayers made. None bidding us safe conduct.
In a woman's back
the butt's thud. Her body gathered, and chucked
into a wagon, with the doors pressed to
sealing the cries that pressed their shapes on them.
        A jolt, and the train started
its riding inward on a plain of snows,

black in a straight line, scissoring this blank in two
erasable and equal whitenesses.

Urine and fear; the fixed erasure over rails;
stench ravelled through hunger. Three days, round my watch.
Food, crammed in our pockets, as we had thought to,
outlasted by shared thirst and hunger. Neither heat nor chill,
stuck in the darkness fixed to earth that paused
over its sullen axis. Occasionally we halted.
Nothing. One further stop, the double note,
someone said, of a plane, many, encroaching.
We were bombed. After, the grinding on. I could see
nothing. My hand in another's, or my arms over her
as if dancing. Sleep, torn at length
by a last halt. Voices in German pulled
and pinned back doors, and she and I stepped through
a huge space, as I dreamed, of emptiness;
                    with here, a bird, pecking
in snow by the svelte guards; their neat
white alpine station, the signal shut across our route.
The station-master in Austrian railway toque.
I thought that I must laugh. We showed our documents.
Barbed, through the snow the high dark live wire, staked.
Fear, my breath dense in me. I smelt
the crushed ooze in the hair of one, that gleamed
shell-like. I stepped back; struck me; stumbling
I thought
I have nothing to show.

The women were stripped before us on the snow,
whiteness skimming a whiteness, dazing me.
Running, as ordered; such election for
what might be seen; what could be seen I watched.
Some fell, with cold. I stood there, but one man
ran to a young girl. Laughter. A nod; the blow
let blood into the snow. Some girls were jabbed
to run, no breath to cry with, and they dropped
abruptly, caught in that soft uniform,
the prick drawn stiff against the trousered leg.
My mother was not seen, nor she I held

through darkness in the train. We were not notable
enough to sift in the first choosings from
this forced community of Poles, and Polish Jews
mixed in with those who sold us, but were yet
included with us. I was glad of this.
For as we were defiling to our huts
I thought I saw one man who lived a block
from us, and who, in hate, discovered us
to those cleansing the soft snowed earth of us.

We left, or dropped. One marched, searching the step
none kept. I could not quite touch her, as we,
too marked to try to seem unnoticeable,
were led, flanked by the guards, into our huts.

Some nights breathed in the shortest days. Air
speckled with carbon. Huts, inlaid with us
in double-layered bunks, continuously re-filled.
We were filed, by district, as though we were a map
sections of which, as the figures melted, emptied
the signs whose grid crammed tightly on more of us.

One night, blood between us. The knot stirred
and came away. She was gone with what
thickened in her. A space came
from a space. Then nothing.
Shalom, some cried.
I sickened. As she could, her mother nursed me; my own
cannot be spoken of. It breathes
into space, flecked with ash.
Peace, some said.
She got that. I shrank on my frame, and clung
to it. Her mother got my food to me,
as others watched us. She sat, touching me,
making flexible a body thinned
by the blood's loss.

An image of a ship sails, with two more,
milk at the salt prow, nearing. The sea

blinks; in its eye a tanker stretched off-shore
turns on itself away. I watched three ships
sail in through Christmas, wind churning the pier,
that flaps the sagging cloth. The masts slip bare.
Men with their bags step through the deck, and swing
onto the stone quay, past the figureless crane.
The hawser's taut, clinched at the capstan's iron.

These images being not deciduous.

STEIN

At times raw soil grazes my eyelids; I
need death to take my shape, a cleric that
might fasten me to it, or, possibly
the doctor's care. One touched me, once; I winced
in perfect health. One fractured the camp.
Each smiled. The first, with powders and advice
tended us. The other, with a rack
of probes, stared at the flesh never anaesthetised.
And guards made sure they had a health unflawed,
half-matt red, like rouge over onion skin.
The snowy bank sweats; smiling slits the heap
of shapely whitenesses, unfastening
the flesh. Formed by some blade a fistula
stops up the blood.
The mouth curves to its mirth. Extended wings
shrink, and the feathery flesh flails, and drops. Some
argued his skill. Flesh struggles, but it yields
a virgin figure of endurance.
He found its point, and did not move past it.
In terror the flesh split, with pain; and ceased.
Or was deformed, unskilfully stitched up.
One of them used up half an hour of pain
helped to her bed. And in my sleep an astral
shape gas-colours, flickering shabbily.
Changed beds. But then the guard discovering her
rising askew from it, beat her. The first five
lining the huts in coupled layers got beaten
every dawn. The blond intelligenced
vigour of the morning guard, my hair
silken as his.

A leaf appears to move
under the eyes. There is more

I told them. God was struck by this, suffering
imagination's growth. I think I glimpsed
a quizzical, wild thought pursing the mouth.
Once I saw how a guard, while shouting at

a boy, pulled from his tunic half a blackened
bread, passed him it, mouthing 'juden juden,
arbeit macht frei.' No one is sure. Some thought
God levered on an elbow painfully off
the floor. And those who on the noon's dot
walked to the chambers and did not walk back
said that the quick of Germany went still
and, listening, heard its cry. I heard nothing.

I stayed my mind over a heap of pistols.

What seemed the point was keeping the whole mind
intact, stopping the flesh from withering.
We were not much to rat or to a thing
that wanted sustenance. I kept two cloths
as handkerchiefs white as I could, white as
is said a whale-bone is. Crushed flat and squared.
They were the whitest square inside the camp.
A tear has impulse, none there; a movement,
a moving out to work, falling to sleep.

But wasn't there, Kye asks, one person there
loved by another. In all this, she said.

The word is scrupulous, and has a hinge
with fear, fatigue, or boredom moving it.
True though. A man, holding together metals, stood
by a woman who bolted them, observed by a guard.
Sometimes in their work they touched. The guard
flinched as he saw this, sometimes hawked, and moved
away, or he would bash one of them. Both
endured the blow; each was of the same town
married in Catholic Poland. They were Jews
with black hair, deicidal.
In the camp there seemed not a second pair
more careful of each other, or, of a stranger, than
these two, aware, at any instant that an unfelt
chipping of care, some little blunting
of sensitivities eroded them.

They were a silent gathering-point for me.
A paired calculus of intent human
scrupulousness linked in our mutual drabness,
by which I, and others, I felt, could measure up
our actions, so, humiliate the self
by suffering the inequalities
of selflessness.
These two bore a seal of privilege, given gladly
despite the thread of equal fairness and unequal
needs common to us.
                        Once the guard found
her working alone; a dram lacking counter-weight
sunk in herself.
No rape; he offered her for her husband white
fresh bread; which she took and gave him.
He ate; it was white and fresh, asking nothing.
But just that portion lifted in him his flesh
a gloss above hers, noticeable to her.
She smiled; some muscle pricked over by a nerve
tensed her. She waited. And the guard approached
with more bread, pricing it. She took the bread
and not its price. He struck her, hard, over the mouth.
She, cupping it to her, dropped. No one was there
watching. This, also, her husband ate. She feels
the cells that once multiplied on hope use
and go from her, as on her arms he touches
the down greying.
Her upper lip grew thin, to him fragile as bone.
It came. A fixed proportion of us to stand
and line the chambers, while the rose sublimes
its shadows of zyklon. He heard, and she.
As she, her flesh weakening shaped her choice
and, as it shaped, chose her life, shading
hers from his. She lay still on her bunk.
Although as he smiled, rising carefully from
beside her body, held by her, she heaped
into a smile all that she could, softening
the face into as much of what they each
had felt. The shadow left her then; that smile
travailed its face for days, hovering like gas

on the mouth, on the eyes.
Such dreams, such exercise of abundance, cover her face.
That little life, Finn said, as if it could
have saved itself. You do not know, Kye answered.

But Finn is listening. Dust at the eye,
and dampened by it, smears its soft expanding
shape over the pupil, smarting it.

A second pair worked underground, and bolted
metal sheets, sleeping in the hut by ours,
as equally crammed and as consistently
sifted by gas. These two met in the camp.
No joy in her. She had coiled her hair, tying it
into a huge, fair, glistening knot, piled heavily.
Her left hand had no middle finger there.
She'd brought to wear a broad belt; buckled brass
hooped up a woollen, grey, stained dress. Round him
as he absorbed her gaze, the air went tight
and fastened him to her.
She had a child by him and it was dead.

No quickness, and no moisture; but a thick
vitality. She was alive, she loved him.
All of her face was thin, and like a cry.
She had a brother here, who hated him.

He had been picked out as gauleiter in
our group, choosing the Jews, a Jew amongst
more Jews; a scholar in authority
with no weight, queer with theologies
wedge-shapedly tapering to a blunted edge,
insensitive as less sharp. He sorted us.
He pre-arranged the sequence that we filed
the chambers in; some cried their needs, he used
a deft and moistureless logic for the queue.
He was in education, it was said;
able to calculate, an integer
of their device, recurring terminally.
He drew the good meat, queued by some hatch that

we did not line and, pliant as a limb,
food, pliancy, and reading melted him.

Smoke rises off the stacks; feathery soot
catches the wire. A man walks, hands catching
his thought between them. Guards rose, noiselessly,
strapped to their rifles. Those who had said 'no,
they would not go', were taken from there.
Some said his ledgering was correct. Gathered
among the next figures was Elsë. Her face
ached with vitality. Yes, she said, death.
It was that. She erased the name she loved
with hers, as the good signs
have it, where there are signs
to speak of.

He stood wiping his hands, his cap in them.
Passing she almost glanced at him. He stood
between us. No turn changed with hers.
                                    Her breath
pressed through us, and stayed
her in us

VI SOME GROWTH

KYE

1.
The moon disposes of
much fierce light, in sky
erupting desolately.

2.
My body and its shape
have no rectitude.

3.
And my limits are these

STEIN

Oh, for some natural
simple propriety

yes yes

From human rectitude
anthropomorphic beasts
work to be rid, and quit.

Yes.

The avocation of
complex and sensuous
imagery deforms

or, sensuously enacts
some subtler honesty.

At home such things thrive.
Domestic truthfulness
sardonic, compact, and pink.

The household turns on
its livid flies. Domestic
deformation clears
itself. Dross softly
falls through the air.

KYE

1.
Hair amasses. Thicknesses
root off the brain,
its shape,
its fineness; helmeting
the skull's bones.

2.
And he advances.
It is a gentle, a grave
absurd insistence, coming
to me, taking
my face in his hands.

Stein kisses
me over the mouth.

Not sex, not near it even.
Thankfulness glowing
from release.

The points of hair. The liquid dots of flesh.

3.
What meaning, Finn asks then, his tone cool,
dabbing the brush lightly, the touch, precise,
what meaning can this have? I did, he says,
and covering his voice the boy's small plea
which once I took for innocence in him,
I saw the images of flesh; rightly
I suffered; isn't that sufficient? Must
I suffer them once more, unlike the dead?
They left, their pain died in them. Through no fault
but patience, we bear some of that in us.
What were we made for? My dead, touching me,
open my care, by right; and as I look
past Adam's shape, it is mine stares through him
at me. That is sufficient, it is all
the grief I need, as I can gather in
my hands to give him.

4.
STEIN

Your little child, as if he could take
his thread of injury, and hugging it
to him, creep off. We show the dead pure gifts
that, living, we did not offer them; our grief
come back is comfort to us. You could give
her love, or if not, gentleness, which is
respect dabbing the pain. So much of care
pressing the dead is simple. Even simpler,
the earth wrapping their flesh, its dampness
insinuating nostrils with a grub, – to scythe
flowers at the waist, that stem the granite vase.
Some generosity returns to us
and with love, disguises our own wounds
as we dress others'. Perhaps if I know this
the mind's not so in dalliance with itself
thinning a pure self to fragility.
The neglected spirit
                    suffering by you,
Finn asked. Yes, I said, promptly, and from you.

5.
KYE

Slowly this young boy put back what
little he had, with care, proffered.

1.

Finn

A voice, as other voices, stilled
by accusation; I find yet
something in me needs hearing.

Wales had me; and it was wet
over familiar stone. Town Hill
hastened my father down it. He flushed
bilges, as the ships came.
Work, indifferent to the peasant
over pitted hills, required him.
Ships vivid with rust cut
the Tawë, rustling ore. Fastened then
under the hill, off-ending
what smelters in South Wales got
and made pig of. The life we gathered
was round a rented table. It was mine,
I did not want.
Out, I begged it. I left my blate
originating root there.

Tarred wood amongst sea-flowers.

Love, oh my love
my gently abandoned roots

nothing in me like those
faces that lean through him

and no more of this.

2.
STEIN

She touched Finn's sleeve, but what was it she touched.

The modesty through Finn glances his cheek.

Yes it is possible, I thought. And felt
my form, touched with her care, increase: a small
insistent rising equilibrium.

She stood shortly, she turned from me.

And tough and lucid, formed
an independent shape.

I breathed night-musk the plants breathed out, which scented
the house. Dark, then,
touching our fear, crept rigorously
between branched spaces.
                         Childlessly the night
comes upon long legs, and puts both arms
over the house, with her placing cups
in our preparation turned
aside for a further thing.

A SHETLAND POEM

At Grobsness, a house
mild-visaged above the sea
had three floors; the roof
and its wood hold.

No other beams.
A minimum of elegance spared
in stone. Twelve slabbed frames
admit all that comes.

Dung stamped hard
onto the floor gorges
the blank mouth of the hearth.
The house fills.

A shelter for beasts
the best they may have had;
when we disgorged
from the steel cavalry, our crofts'

flesh thinned to
water and shards. Wasting
grasses spindled some wool
skeined loose.

The wind staggers itself.
With stone broadcast
on low peat slopes
touching water.

Child-absence, absence of women
and the dank flit
of beasts useless save
to the industrious visitor.

But by what we had
before, not worse;
and the slaughtered had not
this good dirt.

Shouldn't we have, by
a tally cut against nights
chilling inside the moon's
crubb* of frost,

wanted, and got, more than
a pinched nissen hut,
fish, skin flayed, the storm's
goring shove.

The ribbed vessel, with sheep
was lifted, and jiggered
clumsily on rock; a creature
stricken beyond repair.

The doe of the sea.
We were not. But what we were
worked under hundreds
of moons icily lugged,

we were slow asking for.

We got from each laird
the fish's head, the crimson liver;
now we have the whole lot.
But less the dead

the depopulating
war, the multiplying thickness
of the Atlantic magnitudes.
Of the sun, a flake.

A pale ameliorating
glüd† quickening
the coil, in us it stiffens
and presses up in mirth.

crubb circular stone wall within which cabbage seedlings are pro-
tected.
†*glüd* the glow from the lights of a town seen at night through mist.
note The two glossed words are from the Shetland language which
is in effect Icelandic.

The throat lusts for its oils.
Joy, joy – spills, and makes free.
We are going to drain, drain and crush
the spent beer-can.

Civilization eats out
the blood from the heart;
the laboured gratitudes
between us and earth

make a lace-tented shawl such
as our women excruciated from
threads marled round bitterness.

THREE SHETLAND POEMS

1.

In upraised hand, the stone house; its good father
and his flesh began their weakening. A monument
to cared-for-acreage – he leant
through his son, his words urging their release.

For his son they were legal; they were the will, codified.
He listened, his heart not in it. Prescience told him
these things will endure no alteration.

The farmer begged his child to be sparing
with breath. It was slowly done.

In the house a diligence of objects.
Ships replica'd, coin; layered sands in tubes.
And in one authoritative portrait, a dead woman.

The hair dankened.

Your mother, your two sisters; the house
of stone. Promise me you will keep intact
lathe and plaster. Let no maculation spore
any part of this. But, he said, in a smoky whisper
drawing off a little, pulling aside his son as if to command a
    secret,
promise me the most needful – that the mortar
be always skimming the house.

The son smiled, abandoning inwardly
his whole self to its shape.

He sifted the elation, through frost, from
Edinburgh's red stone. In Rose
street the ruthless abundance of waste, the patrimony
trickling in silvered filth along the gutters
of a street mantled with women's breath. A tiny
fish swimming in the island's hospitable voe, he watched
himself agog for the silver hook as it pierced
the dangling worm. He became his father's
whole life-time out-of-date.

2.
If you had to choose, I asked her, which of

them would you have? One tongue, at least,
dickered upon the palate, the words,
like fish in a creel, packed on each other.

In the late summer, its small startling beauty
touching her hair, she answered. Their meanings
skeined together, her words were clear:

I would have both worlds.
But choice forced on me,
I would have the best of each.

Through air sloping past the voe, each still
thing seen, a car rode, and, altering its gait,
reclenched on a slow third; its exhaust
smutched the air, the fine machinery
breathing perfectly.

With a smile she turned from this. Walking up
the low slope, she re-entered her house, and took
to herself her solitary form.

In the summer wind, with no haste in it, the smile
dissolved, and the wind reflated earlier
contours of itself, its tress blowing
out over three miles of water.

3.

Beside a precise, working model of the Unst water-mill
in a corner of the Shetland museum a man
was reading the sharp uncial Hebrew.

As a child, I said to him, as a Jew

He smiled. He closed the book trapping his
fingers amongst its pages.

The hammered tools of agriculture, commercial
and marine activity were pinned, and the integers
of work showed up. An odour from two
centuries breathing irreproachably.

He talked; he would detain me. There was
nothing in it. His words had little
purpose, either Jew or Gentile. Not uncial,
nor cursive, nor anything at all but the acts
of a man wishing to detain another. He shook
my hand. The skin was dry. When
he spoke, it was mild and nasal.

At five Saturday evening our boat moved
from Lerwick drawing thirty-five feet of water.

I could hear the man in the Lerwick museum
with salted, cursive breath, annunciating
Shetland.

SOME WORK

1.
Wide as a man crouching pipes sulphur
a stained shore. In shelving brine
opening, clenching, jellyfish squeeze day
with night: a handful
of electrics.

A tuft of mountain daisy
prods threads in knobby earth perching on what the plough cut
past, white and untoppled.

Two eyes search at the flower's.

The skull caps
its cells, thread to thread. A brain
originating
declensionless.

With, sporadically, a twitch
of arrogance, sprung in neglect;
but no change in him, seen
a third time.

2.
Distantly, the harebell tense
on one foot, clapperless, it wavers
through his eyes, spurts
of blue touching up
intense radial blue.

Seeing this much, his mind
endures a feeling recension.

A machine binds up crops.
Some wheats, and grass-stuffs.

Birds gullet spilt seed.

3.
Finds its way in. Sensitively the brain
ennobled by a chattering flash of muscle
working, droops, reminded of labour
it did and did; the spirit inch by inch
its muscle cramping
on bone, humiliates.

Electrically tremoring, a bird shrikes
in the black, nearly frozen soil
its gold beak and jaw.

4.
He minds again the labourer's
loth, merciful energy, that slices
clay for a green-topped root.

The stubborn life stubbornly
tugs out, lets fall, perhaps, flashing dispersions of creatures, and
    braids
them together in work.

Another's hands turn the wheel skidding
the machine through the brow's rim,
this field bulging with the hill's shape.

This shape, their work takes in.

5.
Each of us one fibre in what he braids.
Feels an aged stained clay skin rankling
its flesh on us; a tithe of succour
from us gets offered.

The light hesitating deliberateness
from old fingers, its hand, stained.

One might shrive a tenth; the act
squats in me:
Do that again, it says.

Yes, the flesh repeats clearly, I will.

6.
Hands, the hands. Salted grease on
the wheel held still whatever that
protrusion, stone, lump, gnarl of root, frail skull
he hits, slurring over.

Dragging the hissing plough
about from the hill's
jagged crown into the rejoicing
bedded broad stretch of loam
foliating spiked oats.

The work, though, the hand:

Have done, it cries, jogging the hoe;
finish up

THREE POEMS ABOUT A SETTLEMENT

1.
I picked up a stone
in the settlement, planted among
trees in an oblong;
sounds brushed onto them touched
the intricate vague mind.

Between trees, some young, or fallen
and partly buried by grasses, I fetched up
a flat stone with marks.
It heartened me. I felt relief
that it had, shaped by hands
and incised on,
come through.
What did it read, in words
gouging a vouchsafe
over bed, or fire?
How shall I
be communicated with,
now, here, between trees? A further scratch
might be enough,
a meaningful incision meant
to show up lastingly.

2.
Finding the settlement
and lying in it.
'It lets us' you said.

A friend not known by you now dead.

By us, a reservoir.
Birds' cries, touching.

The ditch is amulet
circling the hill. Water or blood, away in it.

Once though; that is not known. Once

lust, cold stone; and a few cries
violent with smoke. An intruder
is bashed. And the cry
craves its self
rushing from it.
A dwindle of blood. The bird
hops and sinks.

Amongst trees, and a herd of geese,
those, from unnatural causes, now dead,
patched a life
in flocculent snow.

Militia, the linked, harrying
mail of this kingdom
skimming the earth to break
into fine separate grains
the upturned bands of soil
weaken, dechain, and sink
under the plough.

A chain of mail, harrowing the earth,
left the earth.

How much
forward do we look?
I asked you.

3.
Haste is two roaches, darting
onto the carpet; one
with belly swollen.
Mice nest in the foundations, and pitch a shrunk language
our voices weave through.

Can anxiousness
wean itself?

We are moistened, under trees
by each other, in this settlement.

The stone was flaked to shape, placed, and clustered
a group of heads over
the newly-born.

The breasts' filaments glisten
with milk, and the cry for milk.

But this went, as it does, violently.
Fractured blood is a ditch
full of it, let
by soldiers, with their reasons.

For what? Yet despite this,
an Aenean moment, elate
and suppurating fear.

From between trees hedged by stone,
nothing, no, something: a man
bent, streaming from here with, under
his arm, in skins, a package

that wails. Which is seamed
in the creases, each with terror, to the man
clutching blindly another's child,
running with life

THE MALABESTIA

Malabestia (thus the present name of the village Acaster Malbis, by York) was the name subsequently put onto Richard of Acaster. His actions were an off-shoot of an incident in York which is, despite the City guide-book's coy paraphrases, fairly well-known. In 1190, when Richard I was crusading, barons used the king's absence to erase their indebtedness to the Jews of York by the direct method of slaughter. They stirred up anti-Jewish feeling to the extent that the Jews took refuge in Clifford's Tower. They were offered safe conduct if they agreed to conversion, and some few who took that risk perished. Not all of these few however, since three Jewish women got free, and were baptised. The majority of the eight hundred, however, rather than test the citizens' promises, commited collective suicide. Finally, Richard of Acaster, who was one of the indebted barons, killed the three women, afraid that he might otherwise be forced to fulfil his debts on the king's return. The women were mourned by the local community which regarded them, at least nominally, as Christians.

I

1

At twenty water sinking in me crossed
my flesh;
my soul ramified
into some huge dove, quaking hugenesses
of air
along the North Sea's watery nausea:
a central and preposterous saltedness.
Its sullen magnitudes touched me and flared,
then slid back. My curved woman's flesh
by spiritual fingering was worked
like lace the church refines its edges in.

Grease moistens lowering eyelids; the Lord watches.
Let him; the tenancy is his; I am.

A blank quietness shading foliage
circling itself; a circular morass
of pond with-out. Mud adheres the flesh.
The principle of water stirs through it.

Mud is not much. Placidities of it
collate the still-life in its vacuum,
digesting three lives. The end
came and lay still.

II

1

The naked Malabestia. Wild garlic savours
the church area. Stumbling inside.
In wood, in marble, and, with death, their image
focuses into beatitude.

Baptismal life, sloughing its dried skin,
the paid up souls out from their stone row squawk
in whiteness to an upper clarity
not much fashed with who water a lent soul.

Other go on, renting fecundities
of land glacially flat; who have in fee
stone on it, ale-houses, corn, pigs, and men
let out to hoe the soft muck thickening
an arable. Their strips of northern work
induce a fertile lot. The spider hid
in the grave's corner bells death's quivering sharp
maternity over the life we have.
Some power goes on; marble and wood die off.

2

The Malabestia, naked. Wild garlic, stiffening
the penitential air, its rural church
is bolted, until
the crinkling blare notated for the ear
the dead use, opens it. My Lord: Doomsday.

Get up. The bones clink, and the heaven-forged clasps
fastening them, thud rustlingly onto
dank clay. And what remains of screwed board
squeaks as this resurrection, with force
not imaginable to the flesh,
erects the Malabestia's progeny
into a detailed everlastingness
of what they did.

III

1

Eight hundred Jews in York, fearful of Christ's
demoniacal laity. Labouring men,
with splayed stubby palms,
offer on secular hands baptismal rights
in everlastingness, with temporal
extensions *gratis*. Worth considering.

The church gapes, this impure plenitude
promised it.

The Jews won't. All that church-space gets its breath,
and stone grinds its pure habitude again.

2

Love, oh my love, cut in me, here – slitting
the bleb of flesh, one blade
was beloved by us all.

In common preciousness, the righteous blood
heaps off the mound perching the tower we are in.

Three Jewish women accede baptism
and slip free. Judah's blood liquidifies
the earth since inured to it.

3

Water sprinkles on us; the ceremony
gleams through our hair. Not a drop stays.

Grace reaches for our minds, but thankfulness
releases us. Mother, what is death? Sullen

stillness. Two Gods melt my soul and link
their wraths together in it into one
central and pressuring displeasure.

IV

1   What the Malabestia do

Gentleness moves in wools, and pity is
naked in furs. Thus they tread, their dress
fearful for its riches. Much afraid
my father's patrimony, that the king
did not stoop for,
will accrue to me.

The Malabestia have debts. Who cut
the life ties up the purse strings. Let that come,
if it will. The Malabestia, who might
but will not hunt the gentle hare, and tug
its body quiveringly through the hands.

The gentle hare, the Malabestia.

He nears, closely the blissful sun unfolds
and draws the eyes that get and turn this light
back on itself. The knife thrusts and sticks.

Baptismal life shrieks to his God, our flesh
is thrust away.

Prayers of wood
are said by rote. And beads told off, greasy
with fingering, these soaked in paint slick

with unceasing use. They hiss in tallying
over the wire, clashing the farther end,
beads on abacuses, bearing our souls
in flight across the penitential wires,
fingered by spiritual men. The beads
rest between fingers, but the souls in them
are elsewhere delicately acquired, and tagged.

Our bloods flow; steeled in christian terror
we divide the mud clinging us.

2

My failed desertion, my gently abandoned roots,
oh my love, where are you; if that
is not presumption since
we have not met still. I'll draw on
my self my failed
desertion to meet one God with.

One God, in one sufficiency.

Being Christian, might he conclude
my brief soul, levied over death?

Ah my dear father, my blessed God,
since you are he,

would it have cost you so much to have raised
me in your arms, and brought me, dead, that brief
and necessary distance, to your room?
Its moderately gentle space commends
a sprig naked between my breasts. You did
not place that shape there, just the space confined
itself. A sullen pungent odour breathes
care in the mind, of which love presses from it
renewing much. What space, what terse delays?
Care, oh my love, prompting a fingering
of mercy. May my first God see to this?

IT SAYS

Thinking on my life under
the smoked glass, I come near
its substance. As a man watching
another scraping light
off grass, dropped by the sun
across it. As if
he very carefully thought
which blades he should not
deprive. So that each time
I brood, it is not on
my own love, or another's
merely, since I touch
now, even, the fiction which
in the Talmud speaks
of how a man each night
works at the book. This is permitted.
And each night, his wife
attends him, but not just
because she does not read
the Hebrew. It does not
say if this married girl
is beautiful; each night,
the book insists, this man
brailles at the Hebrew's uncial
text. Here, the story slightly shifts:
it is another night. His wife
weeps lightly, so lightly it is
neither against him nor
upon the Talmud but
for her lacking him.
The Talmud hardly speaks
more, but, as if sun
closed up, momently,
a few scraps, a few
hesitations in grammar, adding
that for the tear she dropped
the man dies.

THERE ARE FOUR OF THESE

1. *Persisting*

As the rounded skin lews
seven clustering berries fruit
a yew's branch-tip.
Fastened to wood, whose sap
slows through fibre, they offer,
by inches wintering through
the year curving from sun,
a fireside the mind
absorbs warmth to the cold
sore lesions by. I took
into me their jovial
separate reds the banked
country road was lit
from hedges by. I was glad
for their distinct warmths, not
their offering, but that I
might take, and never let
each bag of tough fruits
know why I wished to.
As if misery
healed very slightly.
I did not stay, but such red
is cordial in me;
I saw, as I years
since opened this fruit, small
silkily combed seeds
in white nylon-like threads
distinct and oilily
together nestling.

2.

In the lane, dangled berries
of yew ripening a pink,
a lit cheerfulness, as leaves
on the chipped stone sprinkle.
At length, the house,
cut in Palladian
with, for twenty years, life
not forming in it. My eyes
take no comfort from this
and stare at its huge
empty modular.
Only as
half turning, the red,
the whitened red and lit
ripening of berries, as if
hallucinatingly
across my eyes. As though
looked at, and wanted
to be looked at, and touched;
lightening in cold a pink
and clustering cheerfulness,
their bulb-like warmths a consenting
illumination among
unlively greens, specked brown, with dubiously
inactive earth
topping Northumbrian
stone jammed deeply
over a central, molten,
slowly turning
point of crucial fire.

3.
The house climbs up and spreads
its taste into the year.
'my hands, my hands' he said
staring on them, and then
over his lord who watched
his hundred workingmen break
their stone out of his rock.
He had his craft; they had
their labouring gratitudes
helping starvation.

Harmless as a winter tear
the red berry outgrows
strictures of windless frost.

The yew-tree here bares its fruit.

And I am glad of the shapely
heat the mind picks
of these seeds past need
of sun, or care that would
develop between them.

And by them,
two onions sprawled in grass
rotund and sensual,
nestling contiguously.
Who came here, and who put
them here to take the frost's
notched teeth?

4.
Mildness that dews, deforms
in mildews of grown frost.
On glass, on breath; out from
the wood, in spores, bedding
two iron distances.

A locomotive sweats
and whistles: the forward sign,
which is 'enter the junction
triangulated under blue
incessant lamps.'

Northumberland, Northumberland.
The pain, that pain.
'Take it away from me'
you said.
          I am not capable.
That of me which derides
the match flared carefully
or, not even flared
on studs of glued sands,
moves with less warmth to reach
the practising wound inside you.

In Islington, you cover
your floor, where your father
is not, and you live by
the practising, continuous
warmth searching the forms
of reciprocity –
of which it is all you
and not me, and which bares
my hand upon your breast.

Northumberland, Northumberland.

Filaments of wind;
a tarred and plucked sea;
the berries, the fruit, and warmth

hung from a yew-tree, each
disfigures and joins into
an image of madness giving
no warmth and crept onto
by frost that coughs inside
the street-cat's throat.

Disposed and windless
strictures of frost;

your four limbs fold
in sleep's thicknesses.

Come away, come away

ISAIAH'S THREAD

1.

Cry. What shall I cry: flesh is grass.

The billow stiffens; the wheats are no longer supple.

Whom are we to send? One we relish
as fresh image of us; he can petition
the little widower.

Then I said, here am I; send me.

The almighty Father, Prince of the grazed fields.

But I saw the fly, its life webbed.
And crouched on its alphabet a voice, crying,
shall the axe boast against who hews with it.

Go go go, it said. I flew into the earth's rim.

And grew cautious. No indeed, I answered.

2.

The lion sniffs the moor's hair; straw-specked wind
upbraids saplings into the trout-mouthed voe.
Out, it said.

What shall I cry? Cry. Why must people by people
be torn?

Yes, I said.

I undid my hand, and fastening to it
a stone dilapidating from a house, crouched
in the grass's time.

I was astonished. Shall they abuse
the creature melting through the field.

I waited with open eyes. Men automatic
with rifles defiled singly across
the fragrant and depopulating croft.

It is a question, I said, of love, and gripped the stone.

The fly will be appointed, the sweated ox;
and a furred leopard, over the kids it has pastured.

Lie together, grin, creep, pant, assemble;
convene the kingdom.